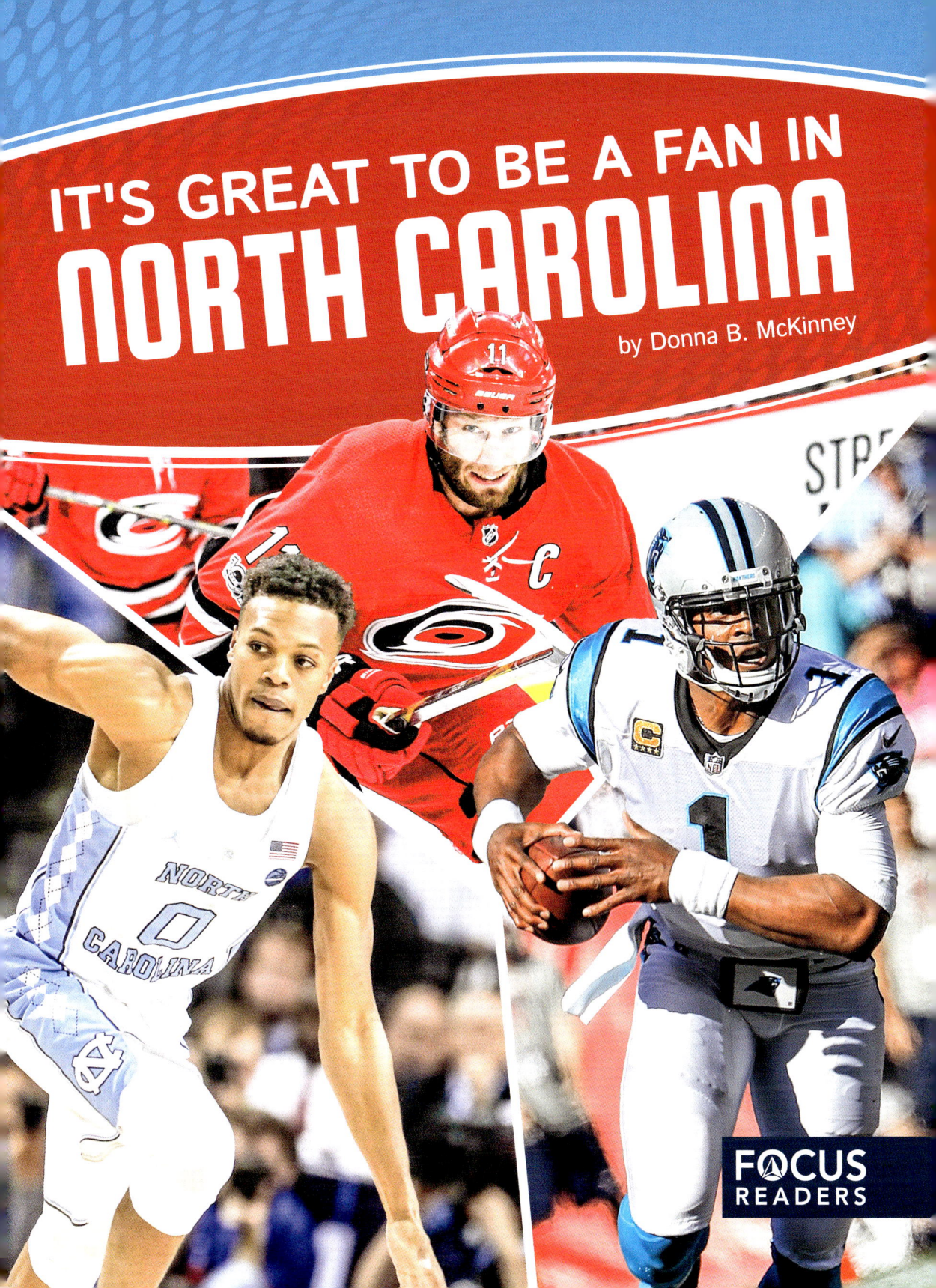

IT'S GREAT TO BE A FAN IN
NORTH CAROLINA

by Donna B. McKinney

FOCUS READERS

www.focusreaders.com

Focus Readers is distributed by North Star Editions:
sales@northstareditions.com | 888-417-0195

Produced for Focus Readers by Red Line Editorial.

Photographs ©: Greg Thompson/Icon Sportswire/AP Images, cover (top), 1 (top); Julie Jacobson/AP Images, cover (bottom left), 1 (bottom left); Winslow Townson/AP Images, cover (bottom right), 1 (bottom right); f11photo/Shutterstock Images, 4–5; Stephen B. Goodwin/Shutterstock Images, 7; Pi-Lens/Shutterstock Images, 9; Red Line Editorial, 11; Brocreative/Shutterstock Images, 12–13; Bob Leverone/AP Images, 15; Butch Dill/AP Images, 17; Ann Heisenfelt/AP Images, 20; Gerry Broome/AP Images, 22–23; Bryan Pollard/Shutterstock Images, 24; Leonard Ignelzi/AP Images, 26; Bob Jordan/AP Images, 29; Action Sports Photography/Shutterstock Images, 30–31; meunierd/Shutterstock Images, 33; John Raoux/AP Images, 34; Andrea Catenaro/Shutterstock Images, 36–37; Brian Westerholt/Four Seam Images/AP Images, 39; iofoto/Shutterstock Images, 42; Michael Conroy/AP Images, 45

ISBN
978-1-63517-934-7 (hardcover)
978-1-64185-036-0 (paperback)
978-1-64185-238-8 (ebook pdf)
978-1-64185-137-4 (hosted ebook)

Library of Congress Control Number: 2018932001

Printed in the United States of America
Mankato, MN
May, 2018

ABOUT THE AUTHOR
Donna B. McKinney is a writer who lives in North Carolina. She spent many years writing about science and technology topics at the US Naval Research Laboratory in Washington, DC. Now she enjoys writing about a wide variety of topics for children and young adults. She is also a contributing writer for *Diversity in Action* magazine, where she writes about science, technology, engineering, and math careers.

TABLE OF CONTENTS

CHAPTER 1

THE TAR HEEL STATE

Sports fans in North Carolina have all the fun. Between the two Carolinas, North Carolina is the one that's home to the area's major league teams. And the fun doesn't end there. North Carolinians also have plenty to cheer for when it comes to college sports, racing, and more.

With an area of approximately 49,000 square miles (127,000 sq km), North Carolina is not one of the largest states. It barely ranks in the top 30.

A snarling panther defends Carolina's home field in Charlotte.

But contained in that land area are a wide variety of landscapes. From the Appalachian Mountains in the west, to the Atlantic Ocean in the east, to the rolling hilly land called the Piedmont in between, North Carolina has it all.

American Indians were the first people to live in what is now North Carolina. The first tribes settled the area at least 10,000 years ago. Eventually, more than 30 tribes made their homes there. They included the Cherokee, Croatan, Pamlico, and many others.

Explorers from Europe first arrived in the 1500s. European settlers built a village at Roanoke Island in 1585. More settlers came in the 1600s. They pushed many native tribes off their land, often through violence.

In 1663, the settlers established the British colony of Carolina. The northern and southern

Lighthouses dot the North Carolina coast. The one at Cape Hatteras is the tallest at 198 feet (60 m).

parts of the colony developed different industries and cultures. The colony officially separated into North and South Carolina in 1712.

In time, North Carolina became famous for its production of barrels of tar, pitch, and turpentine.

These sticky substances came from longleaf pine trees. Boat builders coated their boats with these materials to guard against leaks and worm damage. The tar often got stuck to people's feet. At first, the "tar heel" state nickname was used to make fun of the people who did these jobs. But over time, people began to take pride in the name. And like the tar, the nickname stuck.

After the American Revolutionary War (1775–1783), the United States was officially an independent country. North Carolina became the nation's 12th state in 1789. Two of the state's major industries at that time were cotton and tobacco farming.

Both were harvested primarily through the use of enslaved African people. In 1729, North Carolina had 6,000 slaves. By 1800, there were more than 130,000. The state's first cotton mill

A North Carolina's cotton production doubled to 145,000 bales from 1850 to 1860.

opened in 1813. These mills operated on the cotton picked by enslaved people, who suffered through terrible lives to do so. By 1840, the state had more than 25 **textile** mills.

During the US Civil War (1861–1865), North Carolina sided with the Confederacy, which supported slavery. But North Carolinians were divided on the issue. In fact, approximately 8,000 of them chose to fight for the North. More than 130,000 soldiers fought for the Confederacy.

North Carolina contributed more Confederate soldiers than any other state. Approximately 40,000 of them were killed in battle or died from disease.

By 1919, North Carolina had more industry than most other Southern states. Textiles, tobacco, and furniture were its top goods. The state gained national fame in the 1920s for making furniture in the Piedmont region. By the 1990s, more than nine million hogs lived in the state. This made North Carolina the second-largest pork producing state in the nation.

Despite North Carolina's roots in agriculture, the state's industries are now wide ranging. **Biotechnology**, energy, finance, and information technology all have their place in the state today. In addition, the state is home to more than 50 colleges and universities.

Along with its rich history, North Carolina is home to many great sports, both **amateur** and professional. The state's fans are fiercely loyal to their teams. Sports play a huge role in North Carolina's culture and economy.

NORTH CAROLINA SPORTS MAP

WV

KY

VA

Carolina Hurricanes

GREENSBORO ●

● RALEIGH

Charlotte Motor Speedway

TN

CHARLOTTE ●

Carolina Panthers
Charlotte Hornets

SC

LEAGUE
■ NBA
■ NFL
■ NHL

GA

Atlantic Ocean

CHAPTER 2

PASSIONATE ABOUT PRO SPORTS

North Carolina fans love their professional sports. Today, fans can cheer on major pro sports teams in basketball, football, and hockey. But it all started with pro basketball. Heading into the 1988–89 season, the National Basketball Association (NBA) planned to add four new teams. North Carolina was a natural choice to get one, as the state had a strong fan base for college basketball.

From college to professional, North Carolinians love basketball.

The Charlotte Hornets played their first game in November 1988 at the Charlotte Coliseum. Plenty of fans came out to watch, even though the first three seasons all ended with losing records. But all that losing meant the team got the first overall **draft** pick in 1991. The Hornets used it to select that year's Naismith College Player of the Year, Larry Johnson. In the next draft, the Hornets landed another future star when they took Alonzo Mourning second overall.

Johnson and Mourning gave the team the lift it needed to reach the playoffs. Glen Rice joined the team in 1995. The Hornets reached the playoffs in 1996–97 and again in 1997–98. However, the team never won a championship.

In 2002, the Hornets moved to New Orleans, Louisiana. But North Carolina didn't go long without a pro basketball team. In 2004, the NBA

Charlotte brought back Hugo the Hornet in 2014.

granted Charlotte an **expansion team** called the
Bobcats. Michael Jordan, an NBA Hall of Famer
who grew up in North Carolina, soon became a
part owner of the team. In 2013, the New Orleans
Hornets renamed themselves the Pelicans. So the
Hornets name was available to use in Charlotte.

The team was again the Charlotte Hornets as of the 2014–15 season.

The journey to Charlotte becoming a National Football League (NFL) city started in 1987. Local businessman and former NFL player Jerry Richardson began working to get one of the two new teams that the NFL planned on creating. Richardson's group studied sites in North and South Carolina before choosing Charlotte as the future home of the team. And in October 1993, the NFL owners voted to create a **franchise** in North Carolina.

Dom Capers became the first head coach when the team began playing in 1995. One year later, the Panthers made the playoffs. The NFL named Capers the Coach of the Year.

The 2001 season was a low point. George Seifert was the coach by this time. The team lost

▲ Quarterback Cam Newton is both a good passer and runner.

15 of 16 games. After that disappointing season, John Fox became the coach. And in 2003, Fox led the Panthers to their first Super Bowl. However, the team suffered a heartbreaking last-second loss to the New England Patriots.

The Panthers returned to the playoffs in 2005 and 2008. For the 2011 season, a new head coach, Ron Rivera, arrived. The team also got a new quarterback when **Heisman Trophy** winner Cam Newton joined the team.

Then, in the 2015 season, the Panthers made it back to the Super Bowl. But they lost again, this time to the Denver Broncos. Despite the disappointing loss, Newton was the NFL's Most Valuable Player, and Rivera was Coach of the Year.

The National Hockey League (NHL) also has a strong presence in North Carolina. In 1997, the Hartford Whalers left Connecticut and moved to North Carolina. The team was renamed the Carolina Hurricanes. They played their games in Greensboro the first two seasons while waiting for their new arena to be built in Raleigh.

Their first season was rough, with a record of 33–41–8, and the team struggled to draw fans. Along the way, the team improved, and the fans soon came out to cheer for them.

Ron Francis was the first Hurricanes player to have his jersey number **retired**. Francis had previously played for the Whalers, but he was with Pittsburgh when the Hurricanes came to North Carolina. He returned to the organization in 1998. With the nickname "Ronnie Franchise," he was team captain and a leader on the 2002 team that made it to the Stanley Cup Finals. After he retired in 2004, Francis was inducted into the Hockey Hall of Fame.

In 2006, Carolina defeated the Edmonton Oilers in seven games to win the first championship for North Carolina.

At the end of the 2006 season, the Hurricanes were the NHL champs. This victory made the Hurricanes the first North Carolina team to win a major professional championship.

North Carolina doesn't have a Major League Soccer (MLS) team. But in 2017, the state welcomed a team in the top women's league. The Western New York Flash moved to Cary in 2017 and renamed themselves the Courage. In their first season in their new state, the Courage posted the best record in the National Women's Soccer League (NWSL).

THINK ABOUT IT ◁

What are some of the reasons you think a team would retire a player's jersey number?

CHAPTER 3

COLLEGE BASKETBALL ALONG TOBACCO ROAD

North Carolina offers a wealth of choices to fans of college sports. With more than 50 colleges and universities, the state has teams at the **Division I**, II, and III levels. Student athletes compete in a wide variety of sports including football, baseball, lacrosse, swimming, cross country, and more. But year after year, the college sport that brings the most national attention is basketball.

Duke University's student section at basketball games is known for its passionate fans.

⬐ Cameron Indoor Stadium (first called Duke Indoor Stadium) has been home of the Blue Devils since 1940.

North Carolina's most famous teams play along Tobacco Road. This is not an actual road, but a region where basketball reigns supreme. Duke University, North Carolina State University, the University of North Carolina (UNC), and Wake Forest University can all brag about their historic basketball programs. And the four schools started out within 30 miles (48 km) of one another. In the 1950s, Wake Forest moved 75 miles (120 km) west to Winston-Salem. But there is still a fierce rivalry when these teams play.

Duke's first game at Cameron Indoor Stadium was against Princeton University in 1940. It drew 8,000 fans, 800 short of capacity. People thought the new arena was too big and would never be filled. Cameron had more than twice the capacity of UNC's gym. As time passed, however, interest in basketball grew, especially in North Carolina. The state's arenas were soon packed with fans.

The four schools along Tobacco Road battle it out each year in the Atlantic Coast Conference. And with the campuses being neighbors, all four teams are intense rivals. But many would argue the Duke–UNC rivalry is among the greatest rivalries in sports. Through 2018, Duke had won five men's national titles, and UNC had won six. The UNC women won one national title in 1994.

⚑ North Carolina State coach Jim Valvano led the Wolfpack to a surprise national championship in 1983.

And both UNC and Duke are regular tournament participants.

The list of coaches along Tobacco Road contains some of the all-time greats. In 2017, Duke's Mike Krzyzewski became the first-ever

Division I coach to win 1,000 games. UNC's Roy Williams was not far behind with more than 800 wins. Another legend was Jim Valvano, who led NC State to the 1983 national title in one of the greatest upsets in college basketball history.

The Tobacco Road teams have also fielded some incredible players. Duke has had seven Naismith College Player of the Year winners, including Christian Laettner, Elton Brand, and Lindsey Harding. Tim Duncan won the award for Wake Forest, and Michael Jordan won for UNC. The list of Tobacco Road legends could go on and on.

THINK ABOUT IT ◀

What are some of the qualities that make a great college sports rivalry?

MICHAEL JORDAN

Michael Jordan moved to North Carolina as a young child and grew up in Wilmington. As a sophomore in high school, he tried out for the basketball team but didn't make it. Not one to quit, Jordan kept practicing. The next year he made the team. And from there, he just kept improving.

After high school, Jordan attended UNC on a basketball scholarship. At UNC, he played for the legendary coach Dean Smith. As a freshman, Jordan hit the game-winning shot to give UNC the 1982 national championship. *Sporting News* magazine named Jordan player of the year for his sophomore and junior seasons.

Jordan headed to the NBA's Chicago Bulls in 1984. When Jordan joined the team, the Bulls had a losing record and struggled to draw fans. But that turned around quickly. Fans loved his leaping

△ Both the Tar Heels and the Chicago Bulls retired Michael Jordan's famous No. 23.

ability and acrobatic shots. They didn't mind his amazing scoring ability, either. He played on six NBA championship teams. He won the NBA Most Valuable Player award five times. He is the Bulls' all-time leader in scoring, assists, and steals.

When Jordan retired from playing, he stayed close to the game. Today he is the primary owner of the Charlotte Hornets.

CHAPTER 4

STOCK CAR RACING

North Carolina fans clearly love their teams. But there is another sport that fans flock to see. Stock car racing is the state's official sport. Most fans simply call it NASCAR (National Association for Stock Car Auto Racing). The NASCAR Hall of Fame is in Charlotte. Meanwhile, Charlotte Motor Speedway is in nearby Concord. And dozens of race teams are based in the area.

Charlotte Motor Speedway hosts NASCAR's longest race, lasting 600 miles (966 km).

This makes North Carolina a favorite destination for NASCAR fans.

NASCAR was created in 1948 to govern stock car racing. The first stock cars were almost identical to the everyday cars that people drove on the street. But today, the cars are custom vehicles. They are very different from street cars in cost and construction, but they are made to look similar.

In the early days of racing, the sport was most popular in the southeast United States. Today, however, fans around the world follow the sport. Stock car racing has corporate sponsors and billion-dollar television contracts. More than 1,200 NASCAR races are held each year at tracks all over North America. In addition, the Charlotte Motor Speedway generates numerous jobs and more than $400 million each year.

It is not unusual for racing to become a family business. And there are several NASCAR racing families with North Carolina roots. Perhaps the most famous is the Earnhardts. Ralph Earnhardt competed in the early days of NASCAR. Then his son Dale and grandson Dale Jr. found success as NASCAR drivers. Dale, who earned the nickname "Intimidator" because of his aggressive driving style, died racing in the 2001 Daytona 500.

His wife, Teresa, now runs the racing team Dale Earnhardt, Inc.

The Jarretts are another big name in North Carolina racing. Ned Jarrett gained success as a driver in the 1950s and 1960s. After retiring, he moved to the NASCAR broadcast booth. Following in his father's footsteps, Dale Jarrett is also a NASCAR champion. And like his father, Dale became a broadcaster after he retired as a driver.

The word **dynasty** best describes the Petty family. Lee Petty first competed in NASCAR racing in 1949. Lee's son Richard went on to become one of the most successful NASCAR drivers in history. Lee's grandson Kyle and great-grandson Adam also followed the family business as drivers.

Today, Charlotte Motor Speedway is home to three major NASCAR races each year along with dozens of smaller events. Seating 89,000 people, there's room for plenty of fans to watch the cars race around the 1.5-mile (2.4-km) track that calls itself "The Greatest Place to See the Race."

THINK ABOUT IT ◀

Why do you think children tend to follow their parents in some sports, such as fathers and sons in stock car racing?

CHAPTER 5

SPORTS AT ALL LEVELS

North Carolina fans have their favorite pro and college teams, and NASCAR fans have their favorite drivers. But beyond these more visible sports, players across the state compete in a wide range of lower-level competitions.

From the coast to the mountains, North Carolina has great variety in its geography. The state's coast features approximately 300 miles (483 km) of beaches along the Atlantic Ocean.

North Carolina fans pack minor league parks to see teams such as the Durham Bulls.

Hot summer temperatures there can match those in northern Florida. On the other extreme, the winter temperatures at the top of Mount Mitchell can be bone-chilling. At an altitude of 6,684 feet (2,037 m), the peak set a record low reading of −34 degrees Fahrenheit (−37°C) in 1985. Those western mountains tend to shield the rest of the state from the coldest winter air. So most of the time, the state is a great place for outdoor sports.

Minor league baseball is big in North Carolina. The state has 11 minor league teams. Players also compete in college summer leagues. Two of the most popular minor league teams, the Durham Bulls and the Charlotte Knights, are AAA teams. That means the players are just one step away from reaching the major leagues.

With no Major League Baseball (MLB) team in the state, North Carolina baseball fans won't

▲ The Kannapolis Intimidators were named after the nickname of Kannapolis native Dale Earnhardt.

get to watch those players who then make it to the big leagues. But that is not the case in basketball. Greensboro is a 90-minute drive down Interstate 85 to Charlotte. Greensboro is home to a Hornets minor league team called the Swarm.

The Swarm play in the NBA's G League. They played their first season in 2016.

North Carolina has an NHL team, but it is also home to minor league hockey teams. The state's mild temperatures would cause melting ice at outdoor rinks. That's because the Atlantic Ocean

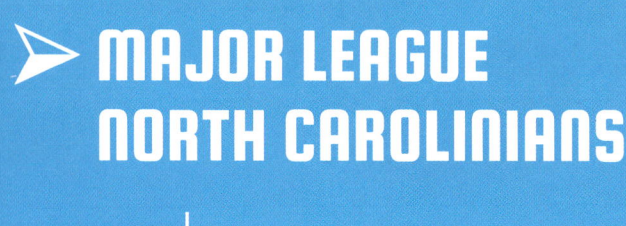

MAJOR LEAGUE NORTH CAROLINIANS

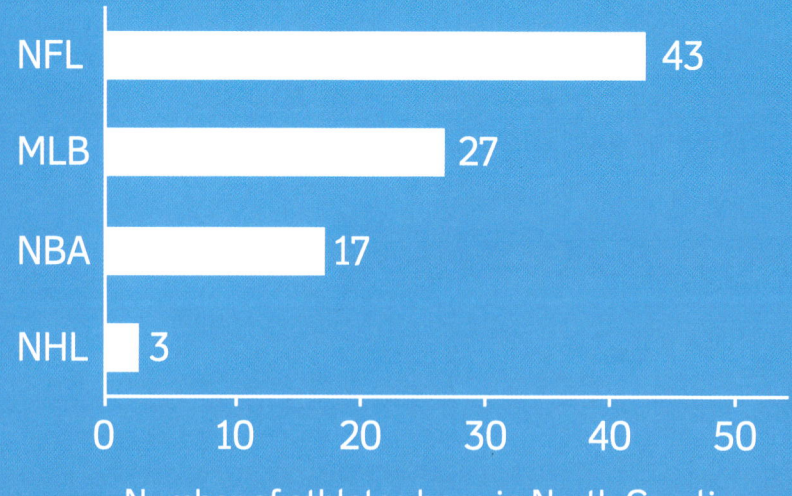

Number of athletes born in North Carolina

Accurate as of January 2018

generally raises the winter air temperatures. But indoor hockey rinks are spread throughout the state. The Charlotte Checkers are the top minor league team for the Hurricanes.

Minor league soccer is present in the state, too. North Carolina FC competes in the United Soccer League. North Carolina even has a pro lacrosse team, the Charlotte Hounds. They were the first pro outdoor lacrosse team in the Southern United States. These sports might not attract the attention of the big-name pro sports. But the teams are well supported by committed players and loyal fans. In some cases, the histories of these teams go back many years and are a big part of their city's culture.

North Carolina's mild temperatures make it a destination for golfers and fans. The state has many great courses that host major tournaments.

Pinehurst Resort has hosted the US Open, the PGA Championship, and the Ryder Cup.

Getting to and from these various sporting events can be an easy drive. North Carolina boasts the second-largest state-maintained highway system in the country. The state has approximately 15,000 miles (24,000 km) of main highways. Other travel options include flying or riding the train. The state has 70 public airports. And there are 3,300 miles (5,300 km) of train tracks. These trains connect major cities such as Raleigh, Greensboro, and Charlotte, along with other smaller cities.

The Tar Heel State has a lot to offer for sports of all kinds. Whether people come to play or to cheer on their team, North Carolina is great place to be a sports fan.

THINK ABOUT IT ◁

What outdoor sport in North Carolina would you most want to play? What is it that you like most about that sport?

KATHLEEN BAKER

When Kathleen Baker was 11 years old, she watched the Olympic Games on television. Her parents noticed that her eyes were glued to the screen during the swimming competitions. Kathleen was already a swimmer, and reaching the Olympics was her goal from an early age.

When Kathleen was 14, her parents moved the family from Winston-Salem to Charlotte so she could train with David Marsh. He was known for his success in coaching Olympic swimmers. Even at that young age, Kathleen loved to practice.

All that practice paid off. Kathleen was **recruited** by the University of California, Berkeley, to compete on its swim team. She even qualified for the 2016 Olympic Games in Rio de Janeiro, Brazil. She showed that she belonged, winning a silver medal in the 100-meter backstroke and a gold medal in the 400-meter medley relay.

⚑ By the age of 20, Winston-Salem's Kathleen Baker was a national champion and Olympic gold medalist.

Kathleen has achieved these dreams while fighting other battles. While still in high school, she was diagnosed with Crohn's, a disease that brings terrible stomach pain and can reduce a person's energy. Kathleen has learned to live with Crohn's and even compete successfully in national and international competitions. By the 2017–18 season, she had already set multiple records at her university.

NORTH CAROLINA

Write your answers on a separate piece of paper.

1. Write a paragraph explaining how North Carolina's weather benefits outdoor sports.

2. Would you rather watch North Carolina's team sports or motorsports? Why?

3. Which was the first North Carolina team to win a major league championship?

  A. Charlotte Hornets
  B. Carolina Panthers
  C. Carolina Hurricanes

4. Why is minor league baseball so popular in North Carolina?

  A. It is the only pro baseball North Carolina has.
  B. The teams have only North Carolina players.
  C. The games last longer than MLB games.

Answer key on page 48.

GLOSSARY

amateur
Someone who is not paid to perform an activity.

biotechnology
A type of biology that is based on technology. Biotechnology is often useful in agriculture, food science, and medicine.

Division I
The top level of college sports in the United States.

draft
A system that allows teams to acquire new players coming into a league.

dynasty
A family or team that is successful for a long time.

expansion team
A new team that is added to a league.

franchise
A sports team.

Heisman Trophy
The award given to the best college football player each season.

recruited
Persuaded someone to attend a college, usually to play sports.

retired
When a jersey number may no longer be worn by another player on a team.

textile
Cloth made by knitting or weaving.

TO LEARN MORE

BOOKS

Foran, Jill. *North Carolina*. New York: Smartbook Media, 2017.

Mack, Larry. *The Carolina Panthers Story*. Minneapolis: Bellwether Media, 2016.

Whiting, Jim. *Charlotte Hornets*. Mankato, MN: Creative Education, 2018.

NOTE TO EDUCATORS

Visit **www.focusreaders.com** to find lesson plans, activities, links, and other resources related to this title.

INDEX

Answer Key: **1.** Answers will vary; **2.** Answers will vary; **3.** C; **4.** A